THE BRAIN WORKS

X-TRAIN YOUR BRAIN

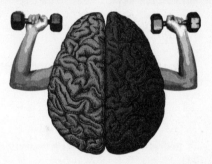

LEVEL 1: BASIC WARM-UP

PUTTING YOUR LEFT AND RIGHT BRAIN TO THE TEST TO ENHANCE ALERTNESS AND MENTAL AGILITY

CORINNE L. GEDIMAN WITH FRANCIS M. CRINELLA, PH.D.

SELLERS
PUBLISHING

DEDICATION

To the memory of Harry Lille

— *Corinne L. Gediman*

Published by Sellers Publishing, Inc.
Copyright © 2012 Sellers Publishing Inc.
Text and puzzles copyright © 2012 Corinne L. Gediman
All rights reserved.

Sellers Publishing, Inc.
161 John Roberts Road, South Portland, Maine 04106
Visit our Web site: www.sellerspublishing.com
E-mail: rsp@rsvp.com

ISBN 13: 978-1-4162-0852-5

Designed by George Corsillo/Design Monsters

10 9 8 7 6 5 4 3 2 1

Printed and bound in the United States of America.

CONTENTS

LEVEL 1: BASIC WARM-UP

The goal of *The Brain Works: X-Train Your Brain* series is to get your brain back to peak performance by rejuvenating specific mental functions before serious decline sets in. It is much easier to maintain mental abilities than to try to regain them, in the same way that it is easier to maintain muscle tone than to try to regain it. A successful exercise program needs to be comprehensive, confidence building, and fun. *The Brain Works: X-Train Your Brain* series is designed to meet all three of these criteria.

The first book in the series, *X-Train Your Brain: Level 1: Basic Warm-Up* provides brain-exercise workouts designed to help you reclaim a younger brain. The exercises are fun, engaging, and stress free. This is the "warm-up" phase of your brain-exercise program. As you advance through the exercise levels of this series, you will build increased brain stamina and resilience. Each level brings you closer to a brighter and healthier brain.

USE IT OR LOSE IT!

Whether you are a busy professional, a multitasking soccer mom, or a retiree, your quality of life depends on the health and resilience of your brain. Using new brain-imaging technology, neuroscientists can see that brain aging begins in our early twenties, and that memory peaks at around age thirty. While this is disturbing news, there is a bright side, and our fate is not sealed.

The last decade has brought a wealth of knowledge about the brain and how it works. Perhaps the most amazing revelation is the brain's miraculous regenerative powers, known as neural plasticity. While once it was believed that brain aging was inevitable, it is now certain that exercising your brain by presenting it with novelty and mental challenges can help ward off mental decline and result in a brighter and healthier brain throughout your lifetime.

Without mental stimulation, however, brain cells slowly atrophy and die, much like body muscles that go unused. When presented with mental challenges, brain cells light up and axons (nerve fibers) start firing. This electrical-chemical activity gets brain cells "talking" to each other. It is this "chatter" that leads to new communication pathways and stronger neuronal connections between brain cells. The result is a healthier, more resilient brain capable of delaying and even warding off dementia and other diseases of the brain. And the best part is that building a brawnier brain is a lifestyle choice.

EXERCISE FOR A BETTER BRAIN

X-Train Your Brain is a brain-exercise program designed by experts in the field. It works on the proven principle that mental muscle, much like physical muscle, can be gained and maintained through an exercise regimen. The program parallels a physical workout routine at your gym, in which you begin by warming up unused muscles, progress to building core strength, and then increase your stamina and accelerate the pace.

There are four exercise levels contained in this series. Each level builds on the last and brings you closer to a better brain.

Level 1: Basic Warm-Up (Stress Free)
Level 2: Building Core Strength (Easy)
Level 3: Increasing Stamina (Moderate)
Level 4: Accelerating the Pace (More Challenging)

X-TRAIN EXERCISE GOAL

Just as a sedentary lifestyle won't keep your body in peak physical condition, a sedentary brain won't retain its mental edge. Retaining peak mental performance is the key to reversing the mental deficits associated with an aging brain, including memory loss, sluggish thinking, and problem-solving confusion.

COMPREHENSIVE

Athletes achieve peak physical performance through cross-training, and we apply this same method for brain athletes. Cross-training your brain makes perfect sense, given the brain's own natural anatomy. The two hemispheres of the cerebral cortex (gray matter) are divided right down the middle into a left hemisphere and a right hemisphere. Each side of the brain is specialized and shows dominance with regard to specific mental processes and abilities. The "left brain" excels at verbal abilities, logic, and linear problem solving, while the "right brain" is adept at visual perception, spatial relationships, and creative problem solving. Collectively these abilities contribute to a fully functioning whole brain. *X-Train Your Brain* targets both left- and right-brain functions and mental abilities, for a comprehensive and total-brain workout.

CONFIDENCE BUILDING

X-Train Your Brain is designed to build confidence and demonstrate your gains. At the gym, progress is easy to see. While last month I was lifting 5-pound weights, this month I can lift 10-pound weights. When I started my workout program, I was doing 15 minutes on the treadmill; now I'm doing 45 minutes.

Level 1 of this series starts off with exercises and games that are fun and easily mastered. This ensures a satisfying, no-stress experience, allowing you to increase your mental stamina at a comfortable, relaxed pace. As you move forward you'll gain the confidence and skills to take on greater challenges. To facilitate success, all of the exercises are preceded by "how to" instructions and examples, so that you know exactly how to approach each puzzle or game.

FUN

Sticking with an exercise program is not easy, as evidenced by lapsed gym memberships and retired exercise equipment sitting in basements. Despite good intentions, physical exercise can become routine, time-consuming, and somewhat boring. That's why only highly motivated, type A personalities tend to stick with it over time.

It's essential to avoid these same pitfalls in a brain-exercise program. The *X-Train Your Brain* series is anything but routine, boring, or time-consuming. Every exercise brings novelty and a new, intriguing mental challenge. Exercises are structured as games and puzzles to ensure a fun and enjoyable workout. And you set your own pace. Success isn't determined by how many exercises you do in a sitting, or how many you get right. Success means bringing some mental challenge and novelty to your brain every day to keep it sharp and agile. The goal is a better quality of mental life.

Since many of the exercises are set up like games, they can be enjoyed by more than one person, or even by competing teams. To turn an exercise into a friendly game, simply add a time limit by which it has to be completed. The winner is the player or team that generates the most responses in a given time frame. Adding timed play to the challenge helps you work on your mental-processing speed, which slows down with age.

BRAIN DOMINANCE
Before you get started, it's interesting to know which side of your brain is dominant. Brain dominance relates to specific mental functions and thinking styles. Most people have a preferred brain-dominance orientation. Your brain dominance will create an affinity for and ease with some puzzles over others. If you are left-brain dominant, you'll definitely enjoy the word games but may struggle with the visual puzzles, and vice versa. You may even be tempted to stick with the exercises that match your brain dominance and skip those that do not. But that would defeat the purpose of a cross-training program, and your gains would be minimized. Remember, the more a mental workout takes you out of your comfort zone, the more novelty it brings to your brain. And the greatest gains come with novelty, because new brain pathways are being tapped.

LEFT-BRAIN CHARACTERISTICS

The left side of the brain excels at language skills, verbal processing, sequential reasoning, and analytical thinking. Individuals who favor this type of thinking are said to be left-brain dominant. They are characterized as logical and rational thinkers capable of excelling in many fields, including science, mathematics, writing, accounting, financial services, teaching, medicine, engineering, research, library science, and computer programming. When problem solving, left-brain-dominant thinkers arrive at the solution or big picture by analyzing and organizing the step-by-step details along the way. They are good forward planners and usually enjoy "talking out" a problem. This brain orientation is compatible with traditional classroom learning, in which students are rewarded for finding the "right" answer.

RIGHT-BRAIN CHARACTERISTICS

The right side of the brain shows dominance in visual-spatial reasoning, random processing (i.e., free association), intuition, perceptual organization, and holistic thinking. Holistic thinkers are able to "see" the "whole" as a picture. They retain information through the use of images and patterns. Perceptual organization, a right-brain-dominant strength, is the process by which the brain takes bits and pieces of visual information (color, lines, shapes) and structures the individual parts into larger units and interrelationships. Individuals who excel in perceptual organization show an ability to arrange color, lines, and shapes into creative works of art, sculpture, and architecture. In school, right-brain-dominant children are whizzes at solving visual challenges, such as puzzles, mazes, block building, hidden blocks, and visual mathematical patterns. In fact, they may be brilliant mathematicians who easily grasp geometry and physics, but be poor calculators who struggle to grasp the linear logic in algebra. Some occupations that attract a right-brain person are inventor, architect, forest ranger, illustrator, artist, actor, athlete, interior decorator, beautician, mathematician, computer-graphics designer, craftsperson, photographer, recreation director, marketing designer, retail specialist, yoga/dance instructor, art director, Web-site designer, fashion designer, and product-package designer.

BRAIN-DOMINANCE SELF-ASSESSMENT

The Brain-Dominance Self-Assessment below will provide insight into whether you are naturally left-brain or right-brain dominant. It will help you understand where your mental strengths lie, as well as what your greatest "mental stretch" opportunities are.

For each item, circle the letter "a" or "b" beside the answer that most closely describes your preference. You must choose either "a" or "b" — you cannot choose both. If you are not sure, consider what your response would be if you were in a stressful, difficult, or new situation. We tend to revert to our natural brain dominance when under pressure.

1 Do you often find yourself following your hunches?
    a. yes
    b. no

2 When you are learning dance steps, it is easier for you to . . .
    a. learn by imitation and by getting the feel of the music.
    b. learn the sequence of movements and talk yourself through it.

3 Do you like to rearrange your furniture several times a year?
    a. yes
    b. no

4 Can you tell approximately how much time has passed without a watch?
    a. yes
    b. no

5 In school, was it easier for you to understand algebra or geometry?
    a. algebra
    b. geometry

6 Do you think logically most of the time about why people behave in a certain manner?
    a. yes
    b. no

7 When given a topic in school, would you prefer to express your feelings through drawing or writing?
    a. drawing
    b. writing

8 When someone is talking to you, do you respond to the content of what is said (word meaning), or to how it is said (feelings, voice pitch)?
    a. what is said
    b. how it is said

9. Is it easier for you to read for the main ideas or to read for specific details?
    a. main ideas
    b. specific details

10. Do you feel more comfortable saying/doing humorous things or saying/doing well-reasoned things?
    a. humorous things
    b. well-reasoned things

11. Are you interested in psychology and holistic healing?
    a. yes
    b. no

12. Do many people think your workspace is messy?
    a. yes
    b. no

13. Do you sometimes act spontaneously or come to premature conclusions?
    a. yes
    b. no

14. Can you always find the right word to describe your feelings?
    a. yes
    b. no

15. Are you objective in your opinions, weighing the facts carefully?
    a. yes
    b. no

16. Are a romantic dreamer or a logical planner?
    a. romantic dreamer
    b. logical planner

17. Are you interested in science and technology?
    a. yes
    b. no

18 If you had to choose, would you rather attend a lecture or go to an artistic event (dance performance, concert, art exhibit)?
    a. lecture
    b. artistic event

19 Do you have the patience to approach a task from different angles until you find a solution?
    a. yes
    b. no

20 Do you like puzzles and word games?
    a. yes
    b. no

21 If you forget someone's name, would you go through the alphabet until you remembered it?
    a. yes
    b. no

22 Have you considered being a poet, a politician, an architect, or a dancer?
    a. yes
    b. no

23 Have you considered becoming a lawyer, a journalist, or a doctor?
    a. yes
    b. no

24 Do you enjoy learning a foreign language?
    a. yes
    b. no

25 Is it easy for you to categorize and put away files?
    a. yes
    b. no

see answers on the following page

Brain-Dominance Answer Key

If your answers to the questions above are fairly evenly distributed between left- and right-brain responses, you are a "whole-brain" thinker with the flexibility to draw on the strengths of both brain hemispheres. If the majority of your responses fall into one or the other brain-hemisphere categories, your natural tendencies are to draw on the strengths of your primary brain dominance as you engage in everyday activities and challenges.

Left-Brain Responses: 1. b, 2. b, 3. b, 4. a, 5. a, 6. a, 7. b, 8. a, 9. b, 10. b, 11. b, 12. b, 13. b, 14. a, 15. a, 16. b, 17. a, 18. a, 19. a, 20. a, 21. a, 22. b, 23. a, 24. a, 25. a

Right-Brain Responses: 1. a, 2. a, 3. a, 4. b, 5. b, 6. b, 7. a, 8. b, 9. a, 10. a, 11. a, 12. a, 13. a, 14. b, 15. b, 16. a, 17. b, 18. b, 19. b, 20. b, 21. b, 22. a, 23. b, 24. b, 25. b

You are now ready to begin your journey to becoming a brain athlete! Remember that the key is to relax and have fun. Did you know that stress kills brain cells? So no stressing. You are about to do something really good for yourself. Enjoy it and feel proud.

PART 1: LEFT BRAIN

CAN YOU SAY IT?

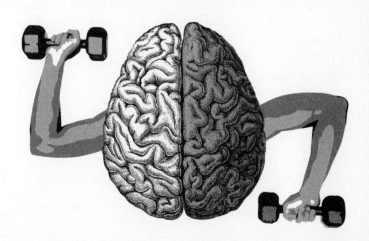

VERBAL EXERCISES

LEFT BRAIN: CAN YOU SAY IT? VERBAL EXERCISES

INTRODUCTION:

The focus of the left-brain exercises is on the left hemisphere's natural proclivity for language skills. Keeping language processing sharp as we age is critical to memory formation, storage, and retrieval. In this left-brain workout, you will participate in a variety of entertaining verbal exercises related to:

LEFT   RIGHT

Logic

Analysis

Sequencing

Linear Reasoning

Mathematics

Language

Facts

Thinking in Words

Words of Songs

Computation

HOW TO PLAY:

The names of colors are often combined with everyday words to form new words. In this game, you will be presented with a palette of color words and a set of noncolor words. Your brain challenge is to form compound words by combining a color word with a noncolor word. The color word can come before or after the noncolor word. For example, if the noncolor word "out" is preceded by the color word "brown" it forms the compound word "brownout," referring to a period of reduced electrical voltage. See if you can create at least 50 compound words by combining the color and noncolor words.

COLOR PALETTE

blue, black, brown, gold, green, pink, purple, red, white, yellow

NONCOLOR WORDS

nose	out	jacket	carpet	code	law	fool's	house	cross
blood	digger	neck	print	lie	mail	ball	fever	jack
grass	bellied	bird	dust	board	cap	sheep	smith	coat
list	fish	bell	heart	lily	eye	thumb	horn	hot
rush	coast	peace	market	true	solid	moon	herring	tape
bread	rule							

ANSWER KEY

COLOR CONUNDRUM

1. BLUE: bluebell, bluebird, blue blood, code blue, bluegrass, blue law, blue moon, blueprint, true blue

2. BLACK: blackball, blackcap, blackjack, blacklist, blackmail, black market, blackout, black sheep, blacksmith

3. BROWN: brownnose, brownout

4. GOLD: Gold Coast, gold digger, gold dust, goldfish, fool's gold, solid gold, Golden Rule, gold rush

5. GREEN: greenhorn, Greenpeace, green thumb

6. PINK: pinkeye, hot pink

7. PURPLE: Purple Heart

8. RED: red carpet, redcoat, Red Cross, red herring, red-hot, redneck, red tape

9. WHITE: whiteboard, white-bread, whitecap, White House, white lie, lily-white

8. YELLOW: yellow fever, yellow jacket, yellow-bellied

OPPOSING PROVERBS

HOW TO PLAY:

Proverbs are expressions that capture the wisdom of the ages in pithy phrases. Yet when examined closely, some proverbs actually offer contradictory points of view. For example, the proverb "A silent man is a wise one" seems to be contradictory to "A man without words is a man without thoughts."

To play, match the number of the proverb on the left to the letter of the contradictory proverb on the right. Write the letter of the opposing proverbs in the spaces indicated in the left column.

1. Knowledge is power. __	a. Too many cooks spoil the broth.
2. Look before you leap. __	b. Out of sight, out of mind.
3. Beware of Greeks bearing gifts. __	c. If you want something done right, do it yourself.
4. With age comes wisdom. __	d. The more things change, the more they stay the same.
5. Nothing ventured, nothing gained. __	e. Life is what you make of it.
6. Money talks. __	f. Fools seldom differ.
7. Great minds think alike. __	g. Ignorance is bliss.
8. Birds of a feather flock together. __	h. He who hesitates is lost.
9. Many hands make light work. __	i. The best things come in small packages.
10. Two heads are better than one. __	j. Better safe than sorry.
11. The only constant is change. __	k. Talk is cheap.
12. The bigger the better. __	l. Opposites attract.
13. Absence makes the heart grow fonder. __	n. Out of the mouths of babes, come wise words.
14. What will be, will be. __	m. Forewarned is forearmed.
15. Cross your bridges when you come to them. __	o. Don't look a gift horse in the mouth.

ANSWER KEY

OPPOSING PROVERBS

1. g
2. h
3. o
4. n
5. j
6. k
7. f
8. l
9. a
10. c
11. d
12. i
13. b
14. e
15. m

HOW TO PLAY:

In this game you will be given five sets of scrambled words. Each of the scrambled words belongs to a specific category. One word, however, does not fit the category. It is a pretender. Unscramble the words to find the pretender. You will be given the pretender category as a clue.

SET ONE: TYPES OF DANCES
PRETENDER CATEGORY: FRUIT

Scrambled	Unscrambled
GTNAO	
ARUMB	
FTXROTO	
IHOHPP	
PLPAE	

SET TWO: ARTIST SUPPLIES
PRETENDER CATEGORY: APPLE ELECTRONIC DEVICE

Scrambled	Unscrambled
OIEPHN	
AACNSV	
ATIPN	
AEELPTT	
ALEES	

ANSWER KEY

CATEGORY SCRAMBLER

Set One: Types of Dances: tango, rumba, fox-trot, hip-hop
Pretender: *apple*

Set Two: Artist Supplies: canvas, paint, palette, easel
Pretender: *iPhone*

HOW TO PLAY:
See instructions on page 19.

SET THREE: ZODIAC SIGNS
PRETENDER CATEGORY: ROCK MINERAL

Scrambled	Unscrambled
RUAUISAQ	
CSEIPS	
IMGEIN	
RUATZQ	
PORRIACCN	

SET FOUR: TYPES OF SPORTS
PRETENDER CATEGORY: SWIMMER GEAR

Scrambled	Unscrambled
OCSERC	
LAOLTBFO	
OGEGLGS	
YGURB	
TNEISN	

ANSWER KEY

CATEGORY SCRAMBLER

Set Three: Zodiac Signs: Aquarius, Pisces, Gemini, Capricorn
Pretender: *quartz*

Set Four: Types of Sports: soccer, football, rugby, tennis
Pretender: *goggles*

CATEGORY SCRAMBLER

HOW TO PLAY:
See instructions on page 19.

SET FIVE: REPTILES
PRETENDER CATEGORY: TYPE OF DOG

Scrambled	Unscrambled
TETLRU	
INAAUG	
DOLEOP	
KEASN	
ORGAILTLA	

ANSWER KEY

CATEGORY SCRAMBLER

Set Five: Reptiles: turtle, iguana, snake, alligator
Pretender: *poodle*

SYNONYM PRETENDERS

HOW TO PLAY:

In this game, you must decide which of two choices is the synonym of the key word and which is the pretender. Circle the choice you feel is the real synonym.

1. Intently
a. resolutely
b. irresolutely

2. Piteous
a. painful
b. sorrowful

3. Relentlessly
a. adamantly
b. pushily

4. Garish
a. colorful
b. tawdry

5. Hypocritical
a. phony
b. judgmental

6. Repulsive
a. smelly
b. offensive

7. Primly
a. scornfully
b. formally

8. Liberated
a. rescued
b. opened

9. Contemptible
a. vile
b. untrustworthy

10. Theory
a. speculation
b. thought

11. Fortitude
a. endurance
b. fearlessness

12. Sporadic
a. periodic
b. unconnected

13. Muddled
a. entangled
b. addled

14. Flank
a. center
b. edge

15. Dumbfounded
a. confused
b. speechless

ANSWER KEY

SYNONYM PRETENDERS

1. resolutely
2. sorrowful
3. adamantly
4. tawdry
5. phony
6. offensive
7. formally
8. rescued
9. vile
10. speculation
11. endurance
12. periodic
13. addled
14. edge
15. speechless

HOW TO PLAY:

Pirates of the Caribbean, starring Johnny Depp, unleashed a passionate interest in "pirates" across a wide gamut of moviegoers. In this game, you will be presented with "pirate lingo." Your challenge is to guess the meaning of each of the pirate expressions. Even if you don't have a clue, use your imagination and make up a meaning. Who knows, you might be right!

SET ONE:
SETTING SAIL

Pirate Lingo	Meaning
1. Fly the Yellow Jack	
2. Give no quarter	
3. Shiver me timbers	
4. Dance with Jack Ketch	
5. A taste of the cat	
6. Crack Jenny's teacup	
7. Parlay	
8. Avast	
9. Cackle fruit	
10. Take a caulk	

ANSWER KEY

PIRATE LINGO

Set One: Setting Sail

1. illness aboard
2. show no mercy
3. expression of surprise
4. hang
5. whipping
6. spend the night in a house of ill repute
7. pirate code of conduct; discussion between disputing parties
8. stop
9. hen's eggs
10. nap

HOW TO PLAY:
See instructions on page 27.

SET TWO:
TREASURE'S IN SIGHT

Pirate Lingo	Meaning
1. Booty	
2. Bucko	
3. Heave to	
4. Jolly Roger	
5. Davy Jones's locker	
6. Ahoy there	
7. Picaroon	
8. Landlubber	
9. Powder monkey	
10. Grog	

ANSWER KEY

PIRATE LINGO

Set Two: Treasure's in Sight

1. pirate treasure
2. friend
3. change the ship's direction into the wind
4. pirate flag
5. bottom of the ocean — watery grave
6. greeting
7. pirate who plunders wrecks
8. person who is clumsy on boats
9. gunner's assistant
10. an alcoholic drink

HOW TO PLAY:

J. K. Rowling's Harry Potter series captured the hearts of young and old around the world. It also spawned a vocabulary of its own. See if you can remember or guess the meaning of the words below, from the fanciful world of Muggles and wizards.

SET ONE:
LEARNING THE SPELLS

Potterisms	English Translation
1. Floo powder	
2. Charm School	
3. Deathday party	
4. Disapparate	
5. Half-blood	
6. Firebolt	
7. Muggle	
8. Parseltongue	
9. Quidditch	
10. Remembrall	

ANSWER KEY

HARRY POTTERISMS

Set One: Learning the Spells

1. powder you throw into the fire, to go wherever you want

2. class at Hogwarts in which you learn about useful spells and charms

3. ghost birthday party

4. leave a place by apparition

5. a person with Muggle and wizard ancestors

6. fastest broomstick model

7. a nonmagical person

8. language spoken by snakes

9. a sport in which wizards fly on brooms

10. a small, glass ball that has smoke inside that turns red when you forget something

HOW TO PLAY:
See instructions on page 31.

SET TWO:
BATTLING EVIL

Potterisms	English Translation
1. Sneakoscope	
2. Spellotape	
3. Time-turner	
4. Amortentia	
5. Veritaserum	
6. Howler	
7. Whomping willow	
8. Mudblood	
9. Animagi	
10. Transfiguration	

ANSWER KEY

HARRY POTTERISMS

Set Two: Battling Evil

1. a device that gives off a whistling noise when someone untrustworthy is near

2. tape used to repair magical items

3. a device which allows wizards and witches to go back in time

4. love potion

5. truth serum

6. letter in which your parents yell at you

7. a tree that hits anything that goes by

8. a person with wizard and Muggle parents

9. wizards who can turn themselves into animals at will

10. the art of changing the form or appearance of an object

How to Play:

In its simplest form, an analogy is a stated likeness between two sets of things that are otherwise unlike. To solve the missing analogy, your first step is to determine the relationship between the first two italicized words. You must then complete the second pairing so it has a parallel relationship. In the example below, the relationship is about characteristics of each species.

Bird is to *fly* as *fish* is to:_____

A characteristic of a *bird* is its ability to *fly*, while a parallel characteristic of a *fish* is its ability to *swim*.

See how quickly you pull up the correct response for each of the missing analogies below.

Set One:
Animal Analogies

1. *Wasp* is to *sting* as *snake* is to _____.
2. *Dog* is to *bark* as *donkey* is to _____.
3. *Duck* is to *webbed* as *horse* is to _____.
4. *Snake* is to *reptile* as *frog* is to _____.
5. *Salmon* is to *fish* as *dolphin* is to _____.
6. *Duck* is to *duckling* as *cow* is to _____.
7. *Lizard* is to *vertebrate* as *cricket* is to _____.
8. *Leopard* is to *carnivore* as *giraffe* is to _____.
9. *Dove* is to *white* as *canary* is to _____.
10. *Zebra* is to *stripes* as *leopard* is to _____.
11. *Polar bear* is to *Antarctica* as *panda* is to _____.
12. *Fish* is to *gill* as *rabbit* is to _____.
13. *Mosquito* is to *six legs* as *spider* is to _____.
14. *Goose* is to *flock* as *buffalo* is to _____.
15. *Cockatoo* is to *feathers* as *camel* is to _____.

ANSWER KEY

ANALOGIES

Set One: Animal Analogies

1. bite
2. bray
3. hoofed
4. amphibian
5. mammal
6. calf
7. invertebrate
8. herbivore
9. yellow
10. spots
11. Asia
12. lung
13. eight legs
14. herd
15. hair

HOW TO PLAY:
See instructions on page 35.

SET TWO:
SPORTS ANALOGIES

1. *Surfer* is to *surfboard* as *golfer* is to _____.

2. *Ballet* is to *slipper* as *hockey* is to _____.

3. *Pitcher* is to *defense* as *linebacker* is to _____.

4. *Pass* is to *throw* as *punt* is to _____.

5. *Baseball* is to *bat* as *boxer* is to _____.

6. *Basketball* is to *period* as *baseball* is to _____.

7. *Hoop* is to *basketball* as *net* is to _____.

8. *Umpire* is to *baseball* as *referee* is to _____.

9. *Crowd* is to *fan* as *team* is to _____.

10. *Biker* is to *two wheels* as *race-car driver* is to _____.

ANSWER KEY

ANALOGIES

Set Two: Sports Analogies

1. club
2. skate
3. defense
4. kick
5. glove
6. inning
7. hockey, soccer, etc.
8. football, basketball, volleyball, boxing, etc.
9. player
10. four wheels

HOW TO PLAY:

Tom Swifties are puns. A pun is a "humorous use of a word, that is pronounced the same as another word, but has an entirely different meaning." Puns are also called a "play on words."

Look at the following example sentence: "I believe there are 527,986 bees in the swarm!" Tom recounted.

The play is on the verb "recounted," which has a double meaning. It means both numerical counting and narrating a set of facts. It is the double meaning that creates the humorous effect.

In this game, you will be presented with a series of Tom Swifty sentences. Each sentence contains a scrambled pun. Your challenge is to unscramble the scrambled puns in italics.

SET ONE:
TAKE IT EASY
In this round, take all the time you want. You can even ask a friend for help.

1. "I need an injection for the pain," Tom pleaded in *n i v a.*

2. "It's the maid's night off," said Tom *l y l e s s p l e h.*

3. "I have a split personality," said Tom, being *r n k f a.*

4. "I'm just an ordinary solider," Tom admitted *l y v a t p e r i.*

5. "I'm losing my hair," Tom *l w d e b a.*

6. "I'll never give up my hounds," said Tom *e d l y g g o d.*

7. "I am waiting to see the doctor," said Tom *t n a p e i t y l.*

8. "We have no bananas," said Tom *r u f i y l e s s l t.*

9. "I will drive you to the emergency room," said Tom *a s i p t o h b y l.*

10. "I'm halfway up the mountain," Tom *g a l l e e d.*

ANSWER KEY

TOM SWIFTIES

Set One: Take It Easy

1. vain
2. helplessly
3. frank
4. privately
5. bawled
6. doggedly
7. patiently
8. fruitlessly
9. hospitably
10. alleged

HOW TO PLAY:
See Instructions on page 39.

SET TWO:
PICK UP THE PACE
Now that you've got the hang of it, see if you can pick up the pace. Think of words that would fit with the theme of the sentence as you begin to unscramble the letters. If the answer doesn't come to you quickly, skip to the next sentence.

1. "I have only clubs, diamonds, and spades," said Tom *l y l e s s e a r t h*.

2. "I've caught Moby Dick," Tom *a i w e d l*.

3. "This boat is leaking," said Tom *u l f y l l e a b*.

4. "I am passionately about camping," said Tom *i n l y e n t t*.

5. "I love hot dogs," said Tom with *h s e l i r*.

6. "I'm glad I passed my EKG," said Tom *e d l y h o l e w a r t h e*.

7. "I will not drink a Chablis," Tom *i h d w e n*.

8. "We'd like a table for two," said Tom without *e r v a s e r n i o t*.

9. "What are you taking pictures of?" Tom *s a n p e d p*.

10. "Mmm, homemade soup," Tom said *i l y u n c a n n*.

ANSWER KEY

TOM SWIFTIES

Set Two: Pick Up the Pace

1. heartlessly
2. wailed
3. balefully
4. intently
5. relish
6. wholeheartedly
7. whined
8. reservation
9. snapped
10. uncannily

HOW TO PLAY:

You will be presented with four sets of grids, each containing five letters. Your challenge is to mix and match the letters to make as many four-letter words as possible.

SET ONE:
CREAM

C		R
	E	
A		M

NEW WORDS:

ANSWER KEY

WORD MULTIPLIER

Set One: Cream

acme, acre, mace, race, came, ream, care, cram, mare

HOW TO PLAY:
See instructions on page 43.

SET TWO:
BREAD

B		R
	E	
A		D

NEW WORDS:

ANSWER KEY

WORD MULTIPLIER

Set Two: Bread

abed, bare, dare, dear, bade, bead, bard, bear, bred, drab, read

HOW TO PLAY:
See instructions on page 43.

SET THREE:
PASTE

T		P
	S	
E		A

NEW WORDS:

ANSWER KEY

WORD MULTIPLIER

Set Three: Paste

apes, pest, step, pats, step, tape, past, peas, east, peat, seat, spat, taps, eats, teas

HOW TO PLAY:
See instructions on page 43.

SET FOUR:
LATER

A		L
	T	
R		E

NEW WORDS:

ANSWER KEY

WORD MULTIPLIER

Set Four: Later

real, teal, tear, tale, earl, rate, late

HOW TO PLAY:

In the English language there exists a multitude of words that mean *group*, and the words can differ depending on the makeup of the group. In this mix-and-match game, your brain challenge is to match a specific group of animals with its collective name. Draw a line to make a match.

SET ONE:

ANIMALS: A–F	COLLECTIVE NAME
1. antelope	a. sleuth
2. bass	b. clutter
3. bacterium	c. float
4. bear	d. paddling
5. cat	e. herd
6. caterpillar	f. skulk
7. clam	g. shoal
8. crocodile	h. army
9. duck	i. culture
10. fox	j. bed

ANSWER KEY

BIRDS OF A FEATHER

Set One: Animals: A–F

1. e
2. g
3. i
4. a
5. b
6. h
7. j
8. c
9. d
10. f

HOW TO PLAY:
See instructions on page 51.

SET TWO:
ANIMALS: G–S   COLLECTIVE NAME

1. gorilla	a. scurry
2. hippopotamus	b. band
3. jellyfish	c. mischief
4. kangaroo	d. parliament
5. lion	e. rhumba
6. mouse	f. pod
7. owl	g. bloat
8. porpoise	h. smack
9. rattlesnake	i. troop
10. squirrel	j. pride

ANSWER KEY

BIRDS OF A FEATHER

Set Two: Animals: G–S

1. b
2. g
3. h
4. i
5. j
6. c
7. d
8. f
9. e
10. a

HOW TO PLAY:

You will be presented with a list of words. Some are spelled correctly, and some are spelled incorrectly. See how quickly you can find the spelling errors and correct them. Circle the misspelled words in Sets One and Two, then write the correct spelling in the box to the right. There is a total of nine misspelled words in Sets One and Two combined.

SET ONE:

Review all of the words, one at a time.

1. acquaintance	
2. Caribbean	
3. indispensible	
4. questionaire	
5. rhythm	
6. inngenius	
7. hypocrisy	
8. ukelelee	
9. dumbell	
10. coliseum	

ANSWER KEY

WORD IMPOSTERS

Set One:

4. questionnaire

6. ingenious

8. ukulele

9. dumbbell

HOW TO PLAY:
See instructions on page 55.

SET TWO:
Review all of the words, one at a time.

1. judgemint	
2. innoculate	
3. accordion	
4. pistachio	
5. pidgeon	
6. hippopotamus	
7. calender	
8. millennium	
9. tomatoe	
10. cemetery	

ANSWER KEY

WORD IMPOSTERS

Set Two:

1. judgment

2. inoculate

5. pigeon

7. calendar

9. tomato

HOW TO PLAY:

In the two sets of this game, you must find the two words —one from the first column, one from the second column — that, if combined, could lead to a common expression, and then write the phrase in the third column below. For example, the words "ace" and "hole," if combined, could lead to the common expression "ace in the hole." In Set One, time yourself to see how long it takes to make all of the matches. Then, for Set Two, see if you can beat your time.

SET ONE:
EASY TIMES   COMMON EXPRESSIONS

puppy	music	
baker's	test	
monkey	wood	
apple	buck	
diamond	bucket	
face	love	
kick	dozen	
knock	business	
nest	down	
pass	eye	
dumb	egg	
acid	rough	

ANSWER KEY

COMMON SAYINGS

Set One: Easy Times

puppy love

baker's dozen

monkey business

apple of my eye

diamond in the rough

face the music

kick the bucket

knock wood

nest egg

pass the buck

dumb down

acid test

HOW TO PLAY:
See instructions on page 59.

SET TWO:

TIME'S UP

pie	kicking
seize	worms
tongue	roses
can	deal
bee	malfunction
bird	wolf
cry	brain
time	day
wardrobe	bonnet
bed	cheek
alive	sky
done	flies

COMMON EXPRESSIONS

ANSWER KEY

COMMON SAYINGS

Set Two: Time's Up

pie in the sky

seize the day

tongue in cheek

can of worms

bee in your bonnet

birdbrain

cry wolf

time flies

wardrobe malfunction

bed of roses

alive and kicking

done deal

HOW TO PLAY:

In this game, you are challenged to combine 20 divided words into 20 whole words by matching the front and back halves of each word together. The words are not necessarily divided by syllable. For example, when you match "TRIU" with "MPH," they combine to make TRIUMPH. Cross off your matches as you go along.

SET ONE:
CARS

NIS	SA	US	OTA	VOL
BU	PEU	OLDS	INFI	FO
VO	AC	SU	BISHI	AT
SLER	FI	CHRY	AU	MER
LEX	TOY	CEDES	SAN	NITI
GUAR	RD	HON	JA	LIN
BARU	MITSU	COLN	DI	URA
MOBILE	DA	GEOT	TURN	ICK

ANSWER KEY

WORD KNITTING

Set One: Cars

Acura, Audi, Buick, Chrysler, Fiat, Ford, Honda, Infiniti, Jaguar, Lexus, Lincoln, Mercedes, Mitsubishi, Nissan, Oldsmobile, Peugeot, Saturn, Subaru, Toyota, Volvo

WORD KNITTING

HOW TO PLAY:
See instructions on page 63.

SET TWO:
FLOWERS

TU	POP	SY	LET	GONIA
SUCKLE	LAC	PRIM	BISCUS	TUNIA
SUN	GAR	WATER	IS	HONEY
CINTH	IR	HI	DAH	THEMUM
PAN	WILLIAM	DAFFO	HYA	PY
DIL	VIO	AS	LIP	LI
ROSE	LIA	CHRYSAN	TER	LILY
DENIA	BE	PE	SWEET	

ANSWER KEY

WORD KNITTING

Set Two: Flowers

aster, chrysanthemum, daffodil, dahlia, begonia, gardenia, hibiscus, honeysuckle, hyacinth, iris, lilac, pansy, petunia, poppy, primrose, sunflower, Sweet William, tulip, violet, water lily

HOW TO PLAY:

A *malapropism* is a comical misuse of a word, attributed to the character Mrs. Malaprop from Richard Sheridan's play *The Rivals*, first performed in 1775. The term refers to the continual act of misusing words or the habitual misuse of similar-sounding words, with a humorous result. Yogi Berra's statement below provides an example of a malapropism.

"Texas has a lot of electrical votes." (The malapropism is the use of the word "electrical" instead of the similar-sounding, correct word "electoral.")

Below are famous malapropisms. Your challenge is to find the malapropism(s) in each sentence, and to replace each one with proper word usage. Circle the malapropisms in the sentences below and write the correct words in the spaces indicated.

SET ONE:
MRS. MALAPROP, *THE RIVALS*

a. "Promise to forget this fellow — to illiterate him, I say, quite from your memory."

b. ". . . she's as headstrong as an allegory on the banks of the Nile."

c. "Sure, if I reprehend anything in this world it is the use of my oracular tongue, and a nice derangement of epitaphs!"

CORRECT WORDS TO REPLACE MALAPROPISMS:

a.

b.

c.

ANSWER KEY

MALAPROPISMS

Set One: Mrs. Malaprop, *The Rivals*

a. "obliterate" for "illiterate"

b. "alligator" for "allegory"

c. "comprehend" for "reprehend"

   "oracle" for "oracular"

   "arrangement" for "derangement"

MALAPROPISMS

HOW TO PLAY:
See instructions on page 67.

SET TWO:
SPEAKERS UNKNOWN

a. "He had to use a fire distinguisher."

b. "Dad says the monster is just a pigment of my imagination."

c. "Isn't that an expensive pendulum around the man's neck?"

d. "Good punctuation means not to be late."

e. "He's a wolf in cheap clothing."

f. "Michelangelo painted the Sixteenth Chapel."

g. "My sister has extracentury perception."

h. "Don't is a contraption."

CORRECT WORDS TO REPLACE MALAPROPISMS:

a.

b.

c.

d.

e.

f.

g.

h.

ANSWER KEY

MALAPROPISMS

Set Two: Speakers Unknown

a. "extinguisher" for "distinguisher"

b. "figment" for "pigment"

c. "pendant" for "pendulum"

d. "punctuality" for "punctuation"

e. "sheep's" for "cheap"

f. "Sistine" for "Sixteenth"

g. "extrasensory" for "extracentury"

h. "contraction" for "contraption"

HOW TO PLAY:
See instructions on page 67.

SET THREE:
ARCHIE BUNKER, *ALL IN THE FAMILY*, TV SERIES

a. "The whole world is turning into a regular Sodom and Glocca Morra."

b. "A woman doctor is only good for women's problems . . . like your groinocology."

c. "I ain't a man of carnival instinctual like you."

d. "All girls go cockeyed during pooberescency."

e. "Irene Lorenzo, Queen of the Women's Lubrication Movement."

f. "Buy one of them battery-operated transvestite radios."

g. "In her elastic stockings, next to her very close veins."

h. "The first priororiry is that I'm the sick one."

i. "To my dear daughter, Gloria Bunker, whom I forgive for marrying the Meathead, I leave my living-room chair as a centralpiece in her someday living room."

j. "Last will and tentacle . . ."

k. "Patience is a virgin."

CORRECT WORDS TO REPLACE MALAPROPISMS:

a.

b.

c.

d.

e.

f.

g.

h.

i.

j.

k.

ANSWER KEY

MALAPROPISMS

Set Three: Archie Bunker, *All in the Family*, TV Series

a. "Gomorrah" for "Glocca Mora"

b. "gynecology" for "groinocology"

c. "carnal instincts" for "carnival instinctual"

d. "pubescence" for "pooberescency"

e. "Liberation" for "Lubrication"

f. "transistor" for "transvestite"

g. "varicose" for "very close"

h. "priority" for "priorority"

i. "centerpiece" for "centralpiece"

j. "testament" for "tentacle"

k. "virtue" for "virgin"

HOW TO PLAY:
See instructions on page 67.

SET FOUR:
LAUREL & HARDY FILMS

a. "We heard the ocean is infatuated with sharks."

b. "What a terrible cat's after me!"

c. "We'd like a room with a southern explosion."

d. "We floundered in a typhoid."

e. "We're like two peas in a pot."

CORRECT WORDS TO REPLACE MALAPROPISMS:

a.

b.

c.

d.

e.

ANSWER KEY

MALAPROPISMS

Set Four: Laurel & Hardy Films

a. "infested" for "infatuated"

b. "catastrophe" for "cat's after me"

c. "exposure" for "explosion"

d. "typhoon" for "typhoid"

e. "pod" for "pot"

HOW TO PLAY:
See instructions on page 67.

SET FIVE:
RICKY, *TRAILER PARK BOYS*, TV SERIES

a. "Worst-case Ontario."

b. "I'm not a pessimist, I'm an optometrist."

c. "Gorilla see, gorilla do."

d. "Survival of the fitness."

e. "Passed with flying carpets."

f. "It's clear to see who makes the pants here."

g. "It doesn't take rocket appliances."

CORRECT WORDS TO REPLACE MALAPROPISMS:

a.

b.

c.

d.

e.

f.

g.

ANSWER KEY

MALAPROPISMS

Set Five: Ricky, *Trailer Park Boys*, TV Series

a. "scenario" for "Ontario"

b. "optimist" for "optometrist"

c. "monkey" for "gorilla"

d. "fittest" for "fitness"

e. "colors" for "carpets"

f. "wears" for "makes"

g. "science" for "appliances"

HOW TO PLAY:
See instructions on page 67.

SET SIX:
THE SOPRANOS, TV SERIES

a. ". . . prostate with grief."

b. "Create a little dysentery among the ranks."

c. "That's right, honey, the sacred and the propane."

CORRECT WORDS TO REPLACE MALAPROPISMS:

a.

b.

c.

ANSWER KEY

MALAPROPISMS

Set Six: *The Sopranos*, TV Series

a. "prostrate" for "prostate"

b. "dissention" for "dysentery"

c. "profane" for "propane"

HOW TO PLAY:
See instructions on page 67.

SET SEVEN:
FAMOUS FOLKS

a. "It is beyond my apprehension." — Danny Ozark, baseball team manager

b. "Listen to the blabbing brook." — Norm Crosby, comedian

c. "This is unparalyzed in the state's history." — Gib Lewis, former Texas Speaker of the House

d. "The police are not here to create disorder, they're here to preserve disorder." — Richard J. Daley, former Chicago mayor

e. "He was a man of great statue." — Thomas Menino, Boston mayor

f. "Republicans understand the importance of bondage between a mother and child." — Dan Quayle, former vice president

g. "Well, that was a cliff-dweller." — Wes Westrum, former New York Giants baseball player, about a close game

CORRECT WORDS TO REPLACE MALAPROPISMS:

a.

b.

c.

d.

e.

f.

g.

ANSWER KEY

MALAPROPISMS

Set Seven: Famous Folks

a. "comprehension" for "apprehension"

b. "babbling" for "blabbing"

c. "unparalleled" for "unparalyzed"

d. "order" for "disorder"

e. "stature" for "statue"

f. "bonding" for "bondage"

g. "cliffhanger" for "cliff-dweller"

PART 2: RIGHT BRAIN

CAN YOU SEE IT?

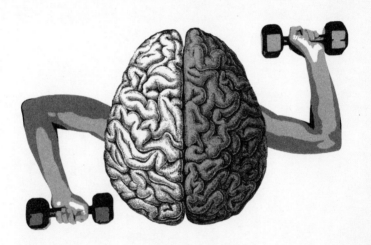

VISUAL PERCEPTION & SPATIAL EXERCISES

RIGHT BRAIN: CAN YOU SEE IT?
VISUAL PERCEPTION & SPATIAL EXERCISES

INTRODUCTION:

The focus of the exercises in this section will be on the right brain's visual-spatial processing strengths. In this workout, your brain will light up as it "sees" the possibilities in the patterns. The puzzles relate to:

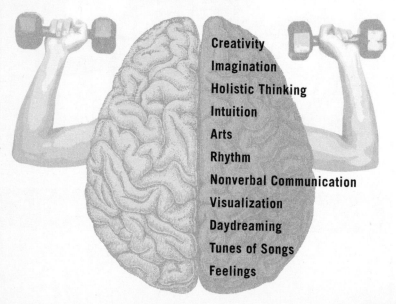

LEFT **RIGHT**

Creativity

Imagination

Holistic Thinking

Intuition

Arts

Rhythm

Nonverbal Communication

Visualization

Daydreaming

Tunes of Songs

Feelings

COMPARE AND CONTRAST

HOW TO PLAY:

In this exercise, you will see two pictures side by side that appear to be exact replicas. But they are not. Your challenge is to identify how the second picture is different from the first. It may have things missing, or things added to it.

SET ONE:
CLOWNING AROUND

Find the five differences between the two images.

ANSWER KEY

COMPARE AND CONTRAST

Set One: Clowning Around

1. missing polka dots on clown hat
2. missing expression lines over clown's eyes
3. missing white accent on nose
4. missing polka dots on tie collar
5. missing white creases in the center of big tie

HOW TO PLAY:
See instructions on page 83.

SET TWO:
SAILING

Find the five differences between the two images.

ANSWER KEY

COMPARE AND CONTRAST

Set Two: Sailing

1. mast tower cages have different number of lines and spaces

2. mast tower cage is suspended by one solid line rather than three

3. medium-size white sail is missing a cross symbol

4. small white sail is missing

5. left side of boat is missing a white window

HOW TO PLAY:
See instructions on page 83.

SET THREE:
QUEEN OF HEARTS

Find the six differences between the two images.

ANSWER KEY

COMPARE AND CONTRAST

Set Three: Queen of Hearts

1. Left inside heart has changed to spade
2. Small flower at top right has a black center
3. Left bodice line of the right-side-up queen is white, not black
4. Small white heart is missing on the upside-down queen
5. Lower lip and cleft-chin mark are missing from the upside-down queen
6. Right outside heart has changed to an upside-down spade

HOW TO PLAY:
See instructions on page 83.

SET FOUR:
DUCKY

Find the five differences between the two images.

ANSWER KEY

COMPARE AND CONTRAST

Set Four: Ducky

1. big duck is missing white back stripes

2. direction of smallest duck is reversed

3. smallest duck is missing black belly stripes

4. medium-size duck has one completely white eye

5. medium-size duck is missing white highlighting on chest

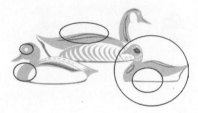

HOW TO PLAY:

In this exercise, you will be presented with a set of images. All but one of the images appear in the mosaic picture that follows. Your brain challenge is to identify the image that is not part of the collage.

SET ONE:
BIRDIE

1

2

3

4

ANSWER KEY

MOSAICS

Set One: Birdie

Image 1 is not part of the collage.

1   2   3   4

HOW TO PLAY:
See instructions on page 91.

SET TWO:
LEAFY

1

2

3

4

ANSWER KEY

MOSAICS

Set Two: Leafy

Image 2 is not part of the collage.

1

2

3

4

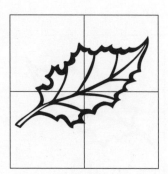

HOW TO PLAY:
See instructions on page 91.

SET THREE:

SUNDIAL

1   2   3   4

ANSWER KEY

MOSAICS

Set Three: Sundial

Image 4 is not part of the collage. The reason is that the "j" in the sun's rays is reversed in image 4 (it appears on the left side rather than on the right side).

1

2

3

4

HOW TO PLAY:

In this brain teaser, you will see a layered image. Your challenge is to identify and circle the *three* singular images that must be combined to create the layered image at the top.

SET ONE:
FALLING LEAVES

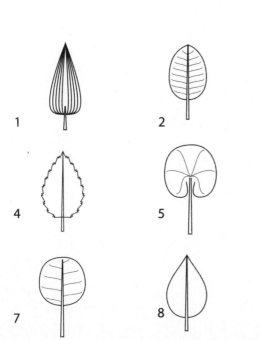

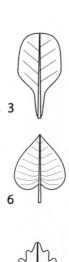

1

2

3

4

5

6

7

8

9

ANSWER KEY

ENTANGLEMENTS

Set One: Falling Leaves

Images 2, 7, and 9 create the layered image at the top.

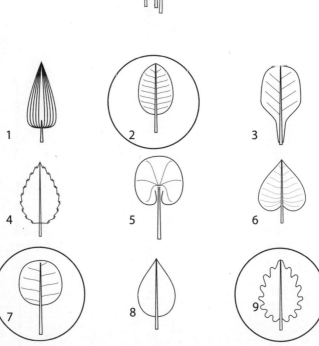

HOW TO PLAY:
See instructions on page 97.

SET TWO:
SHAPE SORTER

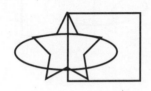

1

2

3

4

5

6

7

8

9

ANSWER KEY

ENTANGLEMENTS

Set Two: Shape Sorter

Images 2, 5, and 6 create the layered image at the top.

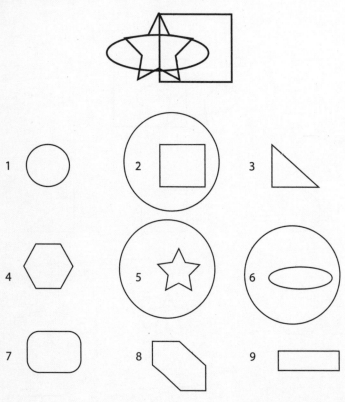

HOW TO PLAY:
See instructions on page 97.

SET THREE:
HANDS

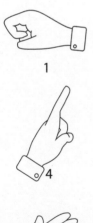

1

2

3

4

5

6

7

8

9

ANSWER KEY

ENTANGLEMENTS

Set Three: Hands

Images 4, 8, and 9 create the layered image at the top.

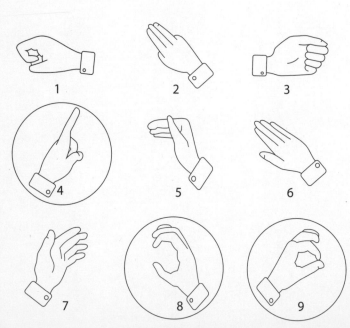

HOW TO PLAY:
See instructions on page 97.

SET FOUR:
TREE SHADOWS

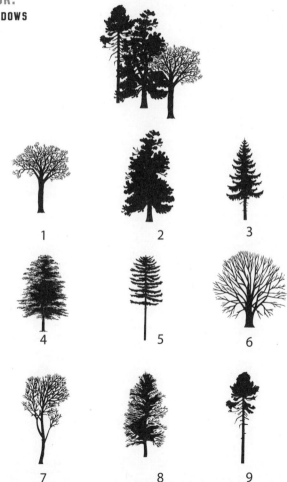

1

2

3

4

5

6

7

8

9

ANSWER KEY

ENTANGLEMENTS

Set Four: Tree Shadows

Images 1, 2, and 9 create the layered image at the top.

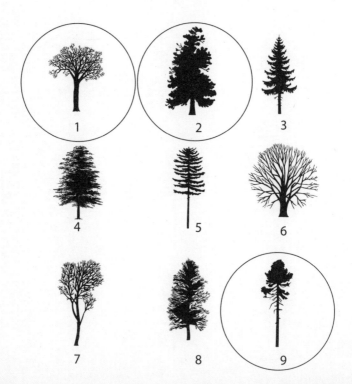

HOW TO PLAY:

In each of the following five sets, you will see a group of images. Try to find the image that is different from the rest. In the example below, can you guess which letter is the odd one out?

C B Q W D

All the letters in the example have curved lines, except for only one letter, which has straight lines. "W" is the odd one out.

SET ONE:

SHIFTING SHAPES

Which shape has different properties from the rest?

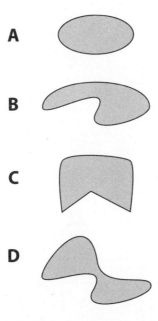

A

B

C

D

ANSWER KEY

ODD ONE OUT

Set One: Shifting Shapes

Shape C is the odd one out because it is the only shape with sharp lines.

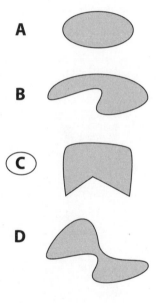

HOW TO PLAY:
See instructions on page 105.

SET TWO:
ROTATING Fs
Which letter "F" does not fit the pattern?

A

B

C

D

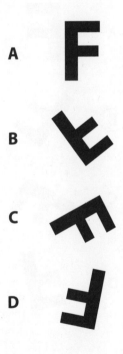

ANSWER KEY

ODD ONE OUT

Set Two: Rotating Fs

B. The second F down is the odd one out because it is an inversion, while all the others are rotations.

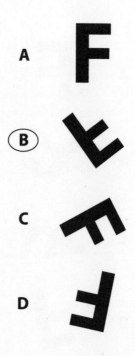

HOW TO PLAY:
See instructions on page 105.

SET THREE:
SMILES & FROWNS
Which face doesn't fit with the rest?

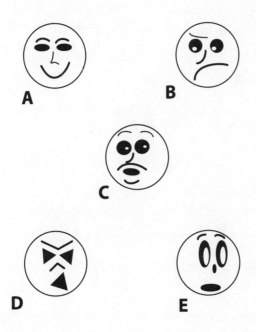

ANSWER KEY

ODD ONE OUT

Set Three: Smiles & Frowns

Face D is the odd one out because it is the only face with all straight lines.

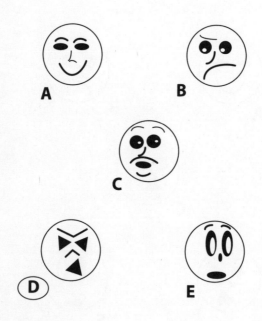

How to Play:
See instructions on page 105.

Set Four:
Bubble Stems
What is happening to the images? Which one doesn't fit the pattern?

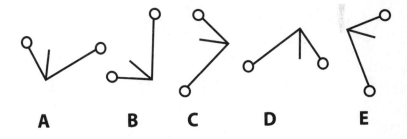

A   **B**   **C**   **D**   **E**

ANSWER KEY

ODD ONE OUT

Set Four: Bubble Stems

Shape C is the odd one out because it is an inversion, while all the others are rotations.

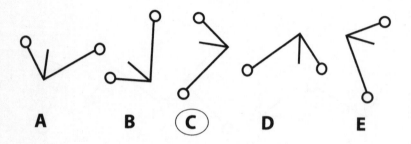

HOW TO PLAY:
See instructions on page 105.

SET FIVE:
UMBRELLA GIRL
Which girl doesn't have a twin?

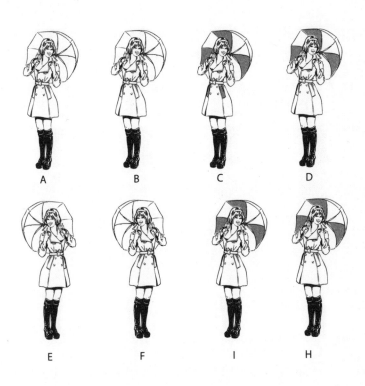

A   B   C   D

E   F   I   H

ANSWER KEY

ODD ONE OUT

Set Five: Umbrella Girl

Umbrella Girl C is the odd one out because she's the only girl with shaded coat pockets.

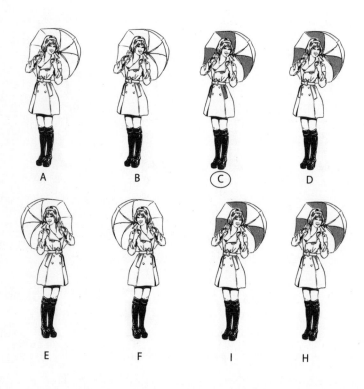

How to Play:

In the next three sets of exercises, your brain challenge is to identify the object that would logically complete the sequence. The key to the sequence is in the visual pattern. Use your left brain to find the "rule" that orders the pattern, and your right brain to see the visual aspects of the pattern. Choose from shapes A, B, C, or D below for the answer. Use the logic questions in each exercise to guide you to the correct selection.

Set One:
Shape Shifting

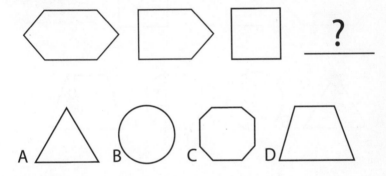

Logic Steps:

1. Consider the question you have to answer: What is the next shape in the sequence?

2. What do you know already? The shapes are different. How? They all have a different number of sides.

3. What is the pattern? The shapes have a smaller number of sides as they progress.

4. What is the answer? Now, trace the pattern in your own mind. What might be the next step in this pattern? Make your best guess before you look at the possible answers. You might be surprised that you can pick it out easily.

ANSWER KEY

NEXT IN LINE

Set One: Shape Shifting

A. The answer is shape A because the shapes on the first line are diminishing by one side at a time.

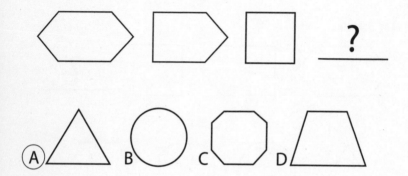

HOW TO PLAY:
See instructions on page 115.

SET TWO:
SIDES & ARROWS

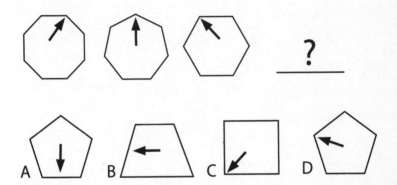

LOGIC STEPS:
1. Consider the question you have to answer: What is the next shape in the sequence?

2. What do you know already? You have seen a puzzle like this before. This one will be a little more challenging. Two things are happening: the shapes are changing *and* the arrow is changing.

3. What is the pattern? The shapes are decreasing in number of sides, and the direction of the arrow is moving.

4. What is the answer? Now, trace the pattern in your own mind. What might be the next step in this pattern? Make your best guess before you look at the possible answers. You might be surprised that you can pick it out easily.

ANSWER KEY

NEXT IN LINE

Set Two: Sides & Arrows

The answer is shape D because every arrow is pointing to a corner in a counterclockwise direction. Since the shapes are diminishing by one side at a time, the correct answer is D, the five-sided shape, with the arrow pointing to the top left corner.

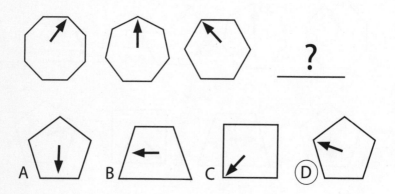

HOW TO PLAY:
See instructions on page 115.

SET THREE:
SPIN THE WHEEL

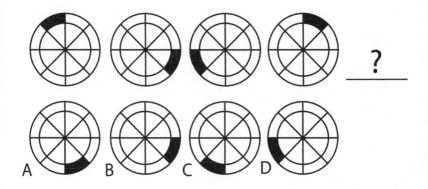

? _____

A   B   C   D

LOGIC STEPS:

1. Consider the question you have to answer: What is the next circle in the sequence?

2. What do you know already? The circle has two rings, but only the outer ring is pertinent to solving this puzzle.

3. What is the pattern? The dark section in the outer ring is moving clockwise.

4. What is the answer? Now, trace the pattern in your own mind. What might be the next step in this pattern? Make your best guess before you look at the possible answers. You might be surprised that you can pick it out easily.

ANSWER KEY

NEXT IN LINE

Set Three: Spin the Wheel

The answer is circle A because the black block in each circle is moving 3 spaces in a clockwise direction.

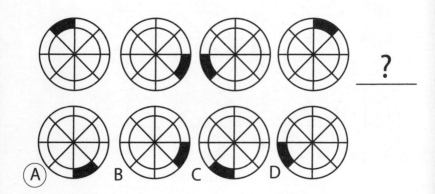

HOW TO PLAY:

In this brain challenge, you must identify the set of shapes that make up the whole image.

SET ONE:
BROKEN CIRCLE

Which set of broken shapes makes up the whole circle?

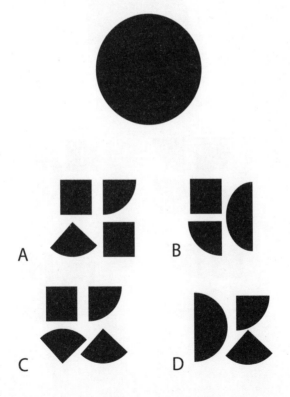

ANSWER KEY

RECONSTRUCTION

Set One: Broken Circle

The correct answer is D.

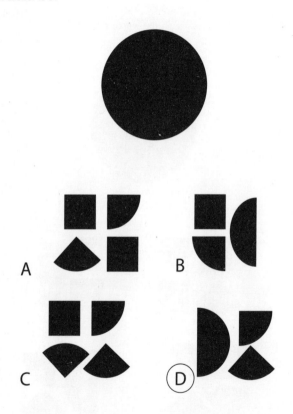

HOW TO PLAY:

See instructions on page 121.

SET TWO:

SPLIT STAR

Which set of broken shapes makes up the whole star?

A

B

C

D

ANSWER KEY

RECONSTRUCTION

Set Two: Split Star

The correct answer is C.

How to Play:

In the following three sets of exercises, your right-brain challenge is to identify the correct match in response to the question posed. To do so, your right brain will need to be in high gear as you twist, turn, rotate, and flip images in your mind to find the right match. Individuals who have a strong right-brain orientation will be able to see the correct match. For the rest of us, the guiding questions will help us by tapping into our left-brain logic.

Set One:
Floored

Which one of the four plans below *matches* the original floor plan above?

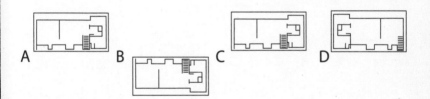

Logic Steps:

1. Consider your goal: to find which floor plan (A, B, C, or D) matches the floor plan at the top.

2. What do you know already? The four floor plans look different. But one of them matches the top one. We need to look for similarities. It might be that a floor plan is rotated and presents a seemingly different view.

3. What is the pattern? Start to look for similar walls. Look for similar placement of the doors. Are the stair steps in the same location and orientation?

4. What is the answer? If you are stuck, trace the original floor plan and move it over the others.

ANSWER KEY

TWISTS & TURNS

Set One: Floored

C. If you mentally rotate the floor plan C 180 degrees, you will see that it matches the floor plan at the top.

HOW TO PLAY:
See instructions on page 125.

SET TWO:
FLOORED AGAIN
Which two four plans below are the *mirror images* of each other?

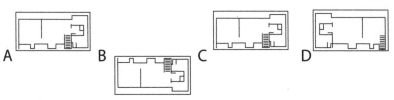

LOGIC STEPS:
1. Consider the challenge you have to solve: to find the two floor plans that are reflections or mirror images of each other.

2. What do you know already? Sometimes developers try to vary the look of a neighborhood by providing two versions of the same floor plan. In one case, they simply flip the existing floor plan to build the mirror image of it. The four floor plans above look different. But one of them is the mirror image of the other. You need to look for similarities.

3. What is the pattern? Start to look for similar walls. Look for similar placement of the doors. Are the stair steps in the same location and orientation?

4. What is the answer? Discard any floor plan that has a feature moved, such as a staircase or a door. This narrows your choices. A piece of transparent tissue paper may be useful to trace a floor plan. Flip the paper over and move it over the other floor plans to see which one matches up. Try rotating the tissue if a match is not apparent.

ANSWER KEY

TWISTS & TURNS

Set Two: Floored Again

A and B. If you mentally flip and then rotate the floor plan B 180 degrees, you will see that the A plan and the B plan are mirror images of each other.

HOW TO PLAY:
See instructions on page 125.

SET THREE:
PUZZLED
Find the correct missing piece of the jigsaw puzzle.

LOGIC STEPS:
1. Consider the challenge you have to solve: One of the puzzle pieces fits in the open space in the partially completed puzzle. Choose the one that fits in the opening. This is difficult because you will not be able to pick up the pieces and try them out.

2. What do you know already? The four pieces look slightly different. But only one of them matches the opening in the puzzle.

3. What is the pattern? The puzzle pieces are very similar. They all have four tabs. They all have grey at the top. Look for what makes them different.

4. What is the answer? Look at each tab independently. Look at the corresponding tabs and blanks in the jigsaw puzzle to see if there is a characteristic that eliminates a piece. Try to eliminate three of the pieces.

ANSWER KEY

TWISTS & TURNS

Set Three: Puzzled

Rule out A because the bottom tab points to the left; it should point to the right.

Rule out B because the grey color is on the wrong side.

Rule out C because the bottom tab is too long.

The correct answer is D.

How to Play:

In this brain challenge, you will be presented with two sets of optical illusions. Optical illusions play tricks with the way your brain receives visual stimuli. For each illusion, a question will be posed. Answering the question below is a key to solving the illusion. The first illusion has a set of logic questions that will help you solve the challenge.

Set One:

Size It Up

Which figure has the larger circle in the middle of it?

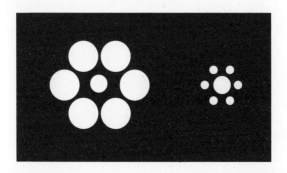

Solving the Illusion:

1. Consider the challenge you have to solve: There are two figures above. Each one has a center circle. You are to determine which of the two center circles is the larger circle.

2. What do you know already? Each center circle is surrounded by six larger or smaller circles. One of the center circles seems larger than the other. You must select the one that truly is larger.

3. What is the pattern? One figure has six outside circles that are much bigger than the outside circles of the other figure. They may be in the illusion to distract us. Ask yourself why they are in the illusion at all.

4. Concentrate your vision on the two center circles. Ignore the outside circles. Which figure has the larger circle in the middle of it?

ANSWER KEY

OPTICAL ILLUSIONS

Set One: Size It Up

Neither one of the inner circles is larger than the other. Cover the outer circles and you will see that the two inner circles are the same size.

HOW TO PLAY:

Optical illusions play tricks with the way your brain receives visual stimuli. Answering the question below is a key to solving the illusion of the "leggy elephant."

SET TWO:

LEGGY ELEPHANT

How many legs does the elephant have?

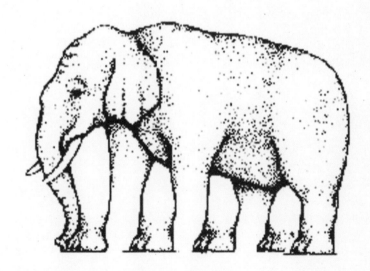

ANSWER KEY

OPTICAL ILLUSIONS

Set Two: Leggy Elephant

The elephant has eight "legs," if you count the images in the foreground (with hooves) and the images in the background (without hooves).

HOW TO PLAY:

Use your right brain to see your way through the four sets of mazes. Trace an unobstructed path through each maze, beginning at the "Start" and ending at the "Finish."

SET ONE:
THE LETTER H

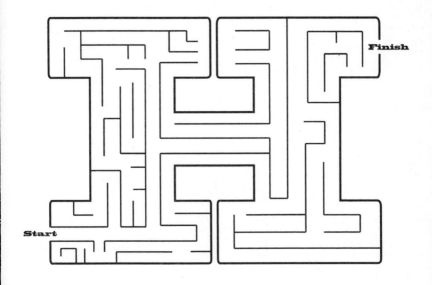

ANSWER KEY

MAZE HAZE

Set One: The Letter H

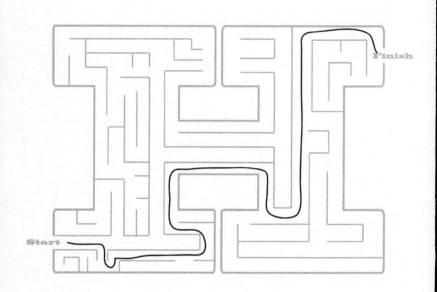

HOW TO PLAY:
See instructions on page 135.

SET TWO:
SINK OR SWIM

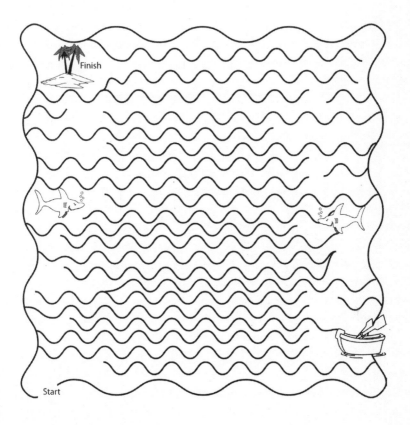

ANSWER KEY

MAZE HAZE

Set Two: Sink or Swim

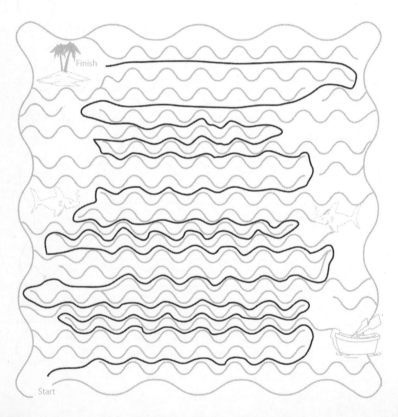

HOW TO PLAY:
See instructions on page 135.

SET THREE:
STARBURST

ANSWER KEY

MAZE HAZE

Set Three: Starburst

HOW TO PLAY:
See instructions on page 135.

SET FOUR:
DIZZY

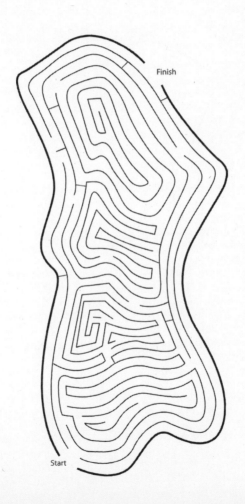

Finish

Start

ANSWER KEY

MAZE HAZE

Set Four: Dizzy

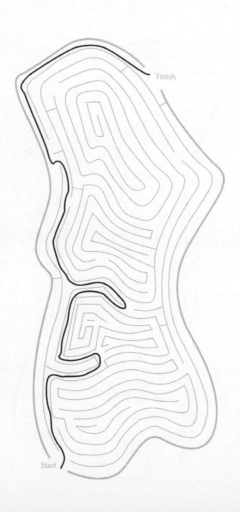

PART 3:
WHOLE BRAIN

CAN YOU THINK IT?

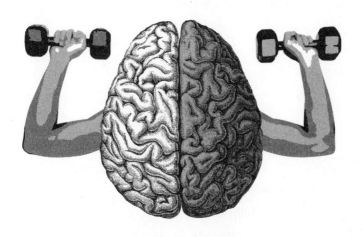

INTUITIVE-THINKING EXERCISES

WHOLE BRAIN: CAN YOU THINK IT?
INTUITIVE-THINKING EXERCISES

INTRODUCTION:

The focus of the exercises in this section is on whole-brain thinking. In this workout, you'll draw on your left brain's analytical processes and your right brain's creative-intuitive processes to solve the puzzles using "out of the box" thinking.

LEFT   RIGHT

Left	Right
Logic	Creativity
Analysis	Imagination
Sequencing	Holistic Thinking
Linear Reasoning	Intuition
Mathematics	Arts
Language	Rhythm
Facts	Nonverbal Communication
Thinking in Words	Visualization
Words of Songs	Daydreaming
Computation	Tunes of Songs
	Feelings

HOW TO PLAY:

AHA! puzzles are those frustrating and challenging puzzles with answers that seem "obvious" — *after* you solve them. However, in order to get to the obvious answer, your brain needs to do some complex parallel processing that synthesizes input from both the left- and right-brain hemispheres. Solving the following three AHA! puzzles requires creative thinking, and the answers often come in a flash of awareness.

SET ONE:
CLIFF-HANGER

This year the owl has very wisely decided to go to sea in a beautiful luxury liner, while the pussycat has chosen to stay behind on dry land and wave good-bye from a nearby cliff top because, being a cat, she doesn't like water all that much. She looks sad because the ship is sailing perilously close to the rocky shore, and she doesn't know what to do to warn it. Quickly now! Take away six straight lines from the pussycat to avert a potential cat-astrophe!

ANSWER KEY

AHA! PUZZLES

Set-One: Cliff-Hanger

Take away the six lines that make up the pussycat's eyes and ears, to leave a lighthouse radiating light.

HOW TO PLAY:
See instructions on page 145.

SET TWO:
COSMIC, MAN!
Can you add the three objects from the far right to the space scene on the left to start a cosmic meltdown? You may place them behind those already in the picture.

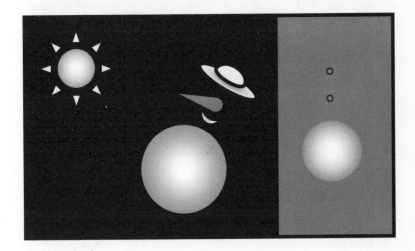

ANSWER KEY

AHA! PUZZLES

Set Two: Cosmic, Man!

Add the objects as indicated to create a snowman.

HOW TO PLAY:
See instructions on page 145.

SET THREE:
SHIP AHOY!
This pirate ship is anchored just off a harbor. What single thing is physically impossible in this picture?

ANSWER KEY

AHA! PUZZLES

Set Three: Ship Ahoy!

The sails would never be up on an anchored boat.

PICTURE PASTE

HOW TO PLAY:

In this game, you will be presented with two boxes of words side by side. Your brain challenge is to arrange one word from each side to form a recognizable compound word. For example, the word combos "car wheel" and "kitchen chair" would lead you to the compound word "wheelchair." If you are artistically inclined and right-brain dominant, you might find it helpful to draw a quick sketch of possible images that the word combos might form.

SET ONE:

playing card: club suit	house arrest

fourth quarter	person's back

human tooth	miner's pick

pile of clothes	horse farm

daily run	one way

fiscal year	black book

ANSWER KEY

PICTURE PASTE

Set One:

1. clubhouse
2. quarterback
3. toothpick
4. clotheshorse
5. runway
6. yearbook

PICTURE PASTE

HOW TO PLAY:
See instructions on page 151.

SET TWO:

garden wall	flower delivery

morning sun	down arrow

cash bar	diving bell

hear ye	say good-bye

person napping	sad sack

betel nut	seashell

ANSWER KEY

PICTURE PASTE

Set Two:

1. wallflower
2. sundown
3. barbell
4. hearsay
5. knapsack
6. nutshell

HOW TO PLAY:

In this game, you will be presented with six sets of four clues each. Your challenge is to use the clue words to guess the hobby for each set.

Set One
guy line
billycan
bivy sack
lean-to

Set Two
tackle box
lead fly
casting
night crawler

Set Three
bench dog
bevel cut
butt joint
cross cut

Set Four
block
fusible web
patchwork
sashing

Set Five
bulb
compost
germinate
grafting

Set Six
penny black
coil
freak
commemorative

ANSWER KEY

WHAT'S MY HOBBY?

Set One: camping

Set Two: fishing

Set Three: woodworking

Set Four: quilting

Set Five: gardening

Set Six: stamp collecting

HOW TO PLAY:

In the following 12 sets, you will be presented with lists containing three items each. One of the items does not belong in the list because it differs in some fundamental way from the remaining two items. Your job is to find and circle the "odd one out" in each set. Here's an example:

Maltese, poodle, spaniel

While all of these are dogs, you would circle "spaniel." Do you know why? That's right — a spaniel has dog fur, while the other two breeds have nonallergenic "real" hair.

Set One: Sports
hockey
football
soccer

Set Two: Composers
Beethoven
Bach
Mozart

Set Three: Edibles
tomato
apple
cauliflower

Set Four: Mixed Bag
Popsicle®
candle
orange

ANSWER KEY

TAKE IT AWAY

Set One: hockey (football and soccer are played with a ball; hockey is played with a puck)

Set Two: Mozart (Beethoven and Bach begin with a "B")

Set Three: caulifower (tomato and apple are fruits)

Set Four: orange (Popsicles® and candles melt)

HOW TO PLAY:
See instructions on page 157.

Set Five: Fishy
blowfish
starfish
jellyfish

Set Six: Worldy
Europe
Canada
Africa

Set Seven: Famous Sites
Mount Rushmore
Yellowstone
Acadia

Set Eight: Government
parliament
socialist
democratic

ANSWER KEY

TAKE IT AWAY, TOO

Set Five: blowfish (starfish and jellyfish are invertebrates)

Set Six: Canada (Europe and Africa are continents)

Set Seven: Mount Rushmore (Yellowstone and Acadia are national parks)

Set Eight: parliament (socialist and democratic are types of governments)

HOW TO PLAY:
See instructions on page 157.

Set Nine: Instruments
telescope
stethoscope
microscope

Set Ten: Sources of Energy
solar
wind
coal

Set Eleven: Fairy Tales
Hansel and Gretel
The Little Mermaid
Snow White

Set Twelve: Anatomy Terms
esophagus
vas deferens
uterus

ANSWER KEY

TAKE IT AWAY, THREE

Set Nine: telescope (the stethoscope and microscope are medical instruments)

Set Ten: coal (solar and wind are renewable energy sources; coal is not)

Set Eleven: *The Little Mermaid* (*Hansel and Gretel* and *Snow White* were written by the Brothers Grimm)

Set Twelve: esophagus (vas deferens and uterus are reproductive body parts)

HOW TO PLAY:

In this game, you will be presented with 12 sets of five clues each. The sets of clues represent characteristics of an object or a type of person. You must put the clues together to identify the person or thing each set describes.

Here is an example:

Clues: *short, green, blade, roots, yard*
Answer: *grass*

Write your answer below each set.

Set One
cold
wet
solid
slippery
translucent

Answer:

Set Two
round
fuzzy
yellow
canned
court

Answer:

Set Three
tissues
sleep
soup
sneeze
fever

Answer:

ANSWER KEY

WHAT AM I?

Set One: ice

Set Two: tennis ball

Set Three: flu

HOW TO PLAY:

See instructions on page 163.

Set Four
leather
locking
rectangular
paper
professional

Answer:

Set Five
wheels
meter
belt
travel
car

Answer:

Set Six
sticky
crystal
granular
sweet
brown

Answer:

ANSWER KEY

WHAT AM I?

Set Four: briefcase

Set Five: taxi

Set Six: sugar

HOW TO PLAY:
See instructions on page 163.

Set Seven
hands
numbers
tock
band
wind

Set Eight
buns
feet
music
pink
slippers

Set Nine
insomnia
pillows
kids
pj's
ghost stories

Answer: Answer: Answer:

ANSWER KEY

WHAT AM I?

Set Seven: watch

Set Eight: ballerina

Set Nine: sleepover

HOW TO PLAY:
See instructions on page 163.

Set Ten
run
leader
term
laws
campaign

Answer:

Set Eleven
window
rack
hot
timer
pan

Answer:

Set Twelve
keys
strings
ivory
sounds
metronome

Answer:

ANSWER KEY

WHAT AM I?

Set Ten: politician

Set Eleven: oven

Set Twelve: piano

HOW TO PLAY:

A "rebus" is a pictorial representation of a name, word, or common phrase. To solve the following sets of six rebus puzzles, you must combine your visual and verbal perceptions to lead you to a creative answer. The example below illustrates how the thought process works. In this example, the word "head" is placed over the word "heels." The black line represents the over/under relationship. Put the visual and verbal clues together and you get the common expression below.

$$\frac{HEAD}{HEELS} = HEAD\ OVER\ HEELS$$

SET ONE:

BUSINESS SENSE

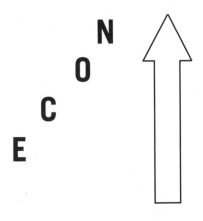

ANSWER KEY

REBUS RIDDLES

Set One: Business Sense

growing economy

HOW TO PLAY:
See instructions on page 171.

SET TWO:
MIXED UP

<pre>
        B
        R
  B R E E D
        E
        D
</pre>

ANSWER KEY

REBUS RIDDLES

Set Two: Mixed Up

crossbreed

How to Play:
See instructions on page 171.

Set Three:
Surprise!

J A C K

ANSWER KEY

REBUS RIDDLES

Set Three: Surprise!

jack-in-the-box

How to Play:
See instructions on page 171.

Set Four:
Not Working

JOBS

IN

JOBS

ANSWER KEY

REBUS RIDDLES

Set Four: Not Working

in between jobs

How to Play:
See instructions on page 171.

Set Five:
It's War

E
L
T
T
A
B

ANSWER KEY

REBUS RIDDLES

Set Five: It's War

uphill battle

How to Play:
See instructions on page 171.

Set Six:
Danger!

COVER

COVER   HEAD   COVER

COVER

ANSWER KEY

REBUS RIDDLES

Set Six: Danger!

head for cover

HOW TO PLAY:

Figure out the relationship among the items in the sequence. Then identify the item that would come next in the sequence. Look at the example below.

S, M, T, W, T, F, ___

The last letter to complete the sequence is "S." Do you know why? That's right. The letters represent the days of the week. The next day in the sequence is Saturday.

WORDS & PHRASES

1. Argentina, Bolivia, Brazil, Chile, Columbia, _____

2. octagon, heptagon, hexagon, pentagon, _____

3. Wyoming, Wisconsin, West Virginia, Washington, Virginia, _____

4. Martin Luther King Day, Presidents' Day, Memorial Day, _____

5. touchdown with 2-point conversion, touchdown with 1-point conversion, touchdown with no conversion, field goal, _____

6. April, August, December, February, January, July, June, _____

7. say, you, by, dawn's, light, _____

8. Obama, Clinton, Reagan, Ford, _____

9. sun, ray, moon, _____

10. Every, Good, Boy, Does, _____

ANSWER KEY

SEQUENCE SOLVER

Words & Phrases

1. Ecuador (South American countries, in alphabetical order)
2. square (names of shapes based on number of sides in decreasing order)
3. Vermont (states in the U.S., in reverse alphabetical order)
4. Independence Day (national holidays, in sequential order)
5. 2-point safety (football points that can be scored, in reverse order)
6. March (months of the year, in alphabetical order)
7. "so" (lyrics to the American national anthem, skipping every other word)
8. Nixon (presidents in reverse order of their administrations, skipping every other president)
9. beam (sun is to ray as moon is to beam)
10. Fine (final word of the mnemonic for the lines of the treble-clef notes)

HOW TO PLAY:

Each of the six riddles that follow contains a concealed truth. Solve the riddle and find the truth. Riddles are not difficult to solve if you use your imagination and trust your intuition. Often the truths hidden in the riddles are quite simple and just require a little "out of the box" thinking.

1. Seventy-eight students are going on a field trip to the Museum of Ancient History. The school rents a big tour bus for the event. The bus holds 79 people, including the bus driver. Why are there not enough seats on the day of the event?

2. People are gathered at night in front of their neighbors' homes. They are all ages and are holding sheets of paper in their hands. They spend a few minutes in front of each house after the homeowner comes to the door. They do not hand out the paper, and sometimes the homeowner joins them in going to the next house. Who are these people?

3. Susan comes home late for dinner to find an angry partner who says he's been waiting with food on the table for three hours. Salad, soup, and bread are sitting on a table with tall candles burning brightly. How does Susan know that her husband is exaggerating how long he's been waiting?

ANSWER KEY

MINI MYSTERIES

1. No seat for the teacher

2. Christmas carolers

3. The candles are barely burned down.

HOW TO PLAY:
See instructions on page 185.

4. Jamal spends an hour with his whole body suspended horizontally above the ground. There are no ropes or objects holding him up. While he's suspended, he is exercising. Usually, he wears a cap on his head and funny-looking eyewear. What is he doing?

5. Kevin finds his daughter in the kitchen crying. When he asks her what's wrong, she responds in a normal-sounding voice, "Absolutely nothing. I'm just making vegetable soup." Why might she be crying?

6. Eleven-year-old Janie delivers the paper in her neighborhood every morning. She puts on special shoes to speed up her job, but she doesn't walk or run on her route. How does Janie travel?

ANSWER KEY

MINI MYSTERIES

4. swimming

5. She is peeling onions.

6. She is roller-skating.

HOW TO PLAY:

Link the following items from small to big by drawing a continuous connecting line, starting with the smallest item and ending with the largest. Once you start, you cannot go back. If you think you made an error, just continue. You still have a chance to get most of them right. Before you begin, identify the first and last items in the sequence.

1. berry

2. snowman

3. pineapple

4. chipmunk

5. grape

6. rabbit

7. grain of sand

8. fox

9. toddler

10. kitten

11. lemon

12. ladybug

13. bear

ANSWER KEY

SMALL TO BIG

1. grain of sand
2. ladybug
3. berry
4. grape
5. lemon
6. chipmunk
7. kitten
8. pineapple
9. rabbit
10. fox
11. toddler
12. snowman
13. bear

ACKNOWLEDGMENTS

I want to thank the following people who made this book posible — from Sellers Publishing: Publishing Director Robin Haywod; Editor in Chief, Books, Mark Chimsky; Managing Editor Mary Baldwin; and Production Editor Charlotte Cromwell; as well a proofreader Renee Rooks Cooley; book designer George Corsio, Design Monsters; designer Bill Becker, BC Graphics; my ager, Coleen O'Shea, Allen O'Shea Literary Agency; and Dr. FranciM. Crinella, neuropsychology contributor. I would also like to thak my friends and family for their continued support and encourageent.

— *Corinne L. Geman*